Edwin McLean

MINIATURES

BOOK 1

Notes from the Publisher

Composers In Focus is a series of original piano collections celebrating the creative artistry of contemporary composers. It is through the work of these composers that the piano teaching repertoire is enlarged and enhanced.

It is my hope that students, teachers, and all others who experience this music will be enriched and inspired.

Frank J. Hackinson

Frank J. Hackinson, Publisher

Notes from the Composer

Miniatures, Book 1 is an artistic collection of elementary piano solos for students of all ages. The hands center around five-finger positions, with some lateral movement. No eighth notes are used. Accidentals are favored instead of key signatures.

Miniatures, Book 1 features a wide variety of images and moods. The compositions are modern without being dissonant. While this collection may be used to supplement any method, it is also designed as a pathway to the standard classical literature.

Edwin McLean

Edwin McLean

Contents

Speak Up, Please!

Edwin McLean

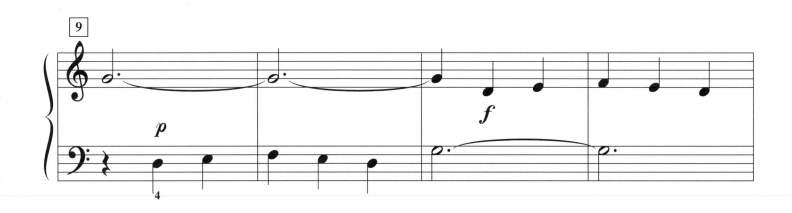

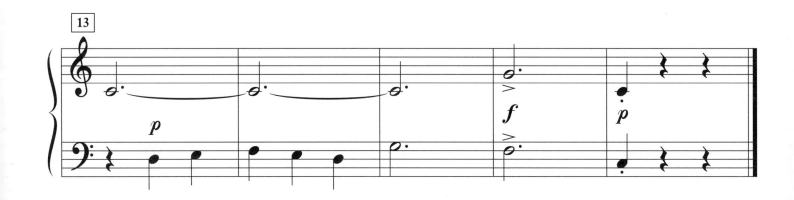

Island Breeze

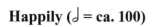

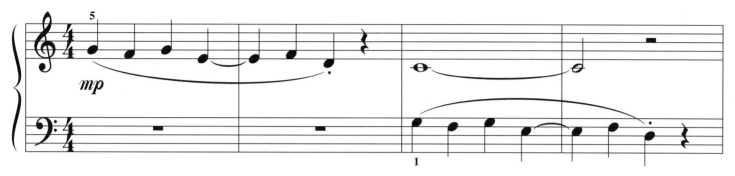

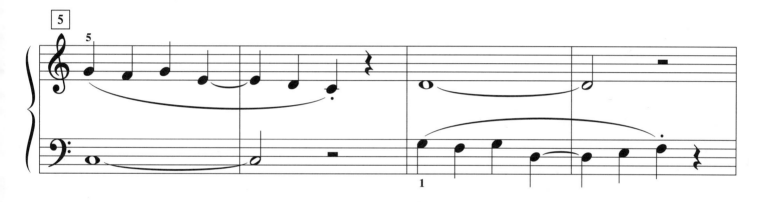

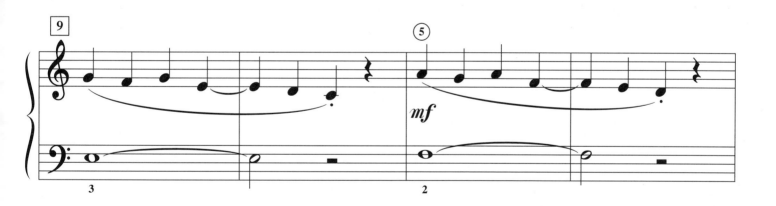

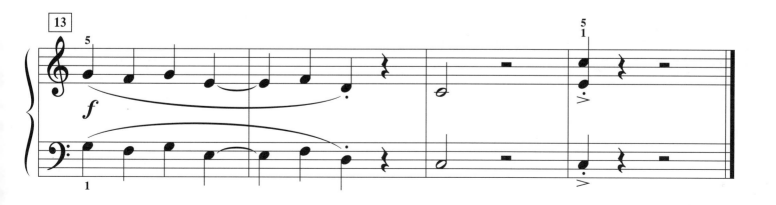

Hurry!

Quickly (♩ = 96 or faster)

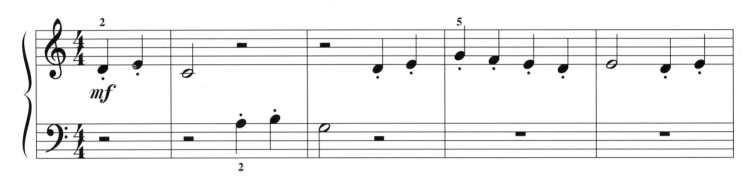

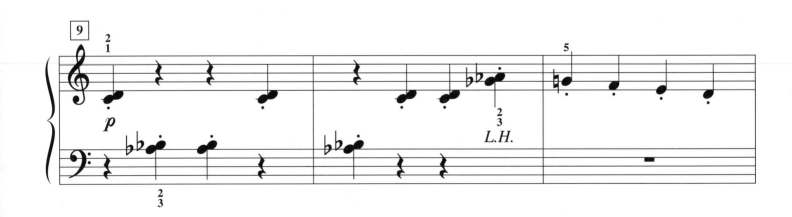

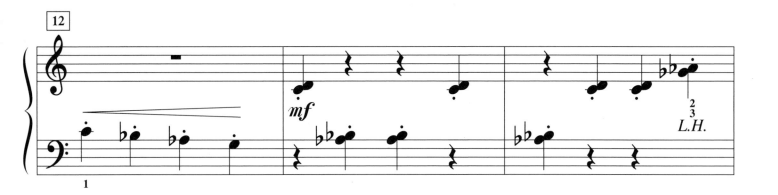

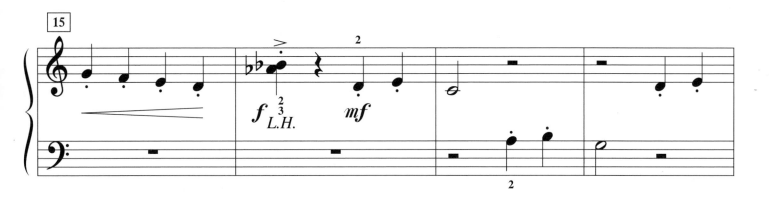

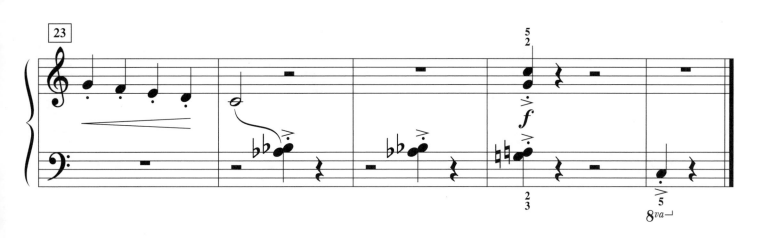

Rain, Rain...

Thoughtfully ($\quarternote$ = ca. 96)

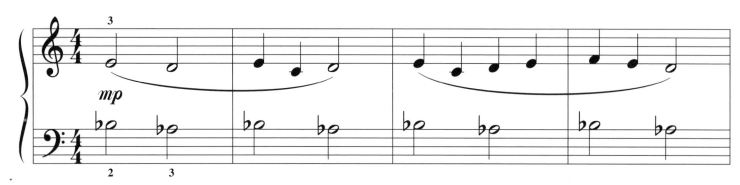

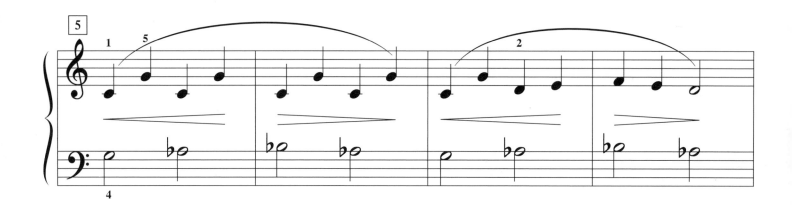

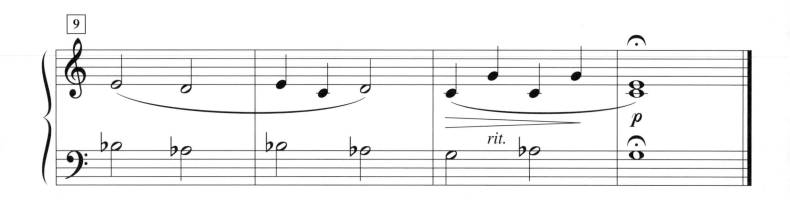

Medieval Dance

With motion (♩ = ca. 80)

R.H. 8va (2nd time only)

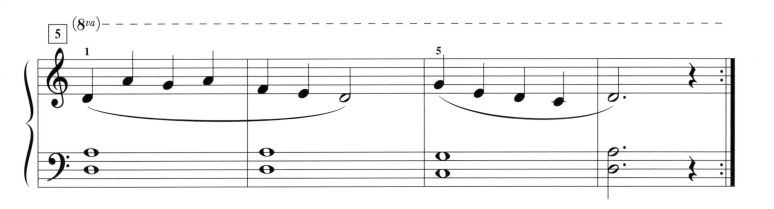

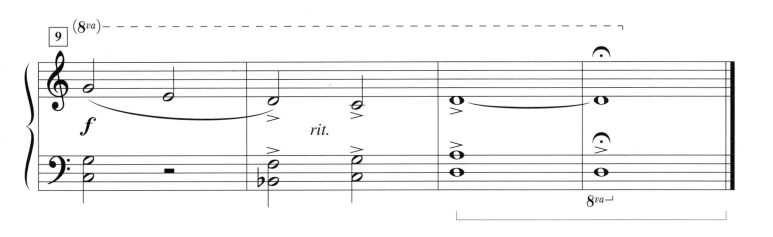

Early Morning Sky

Calmly ($\:$ = ca. 96)

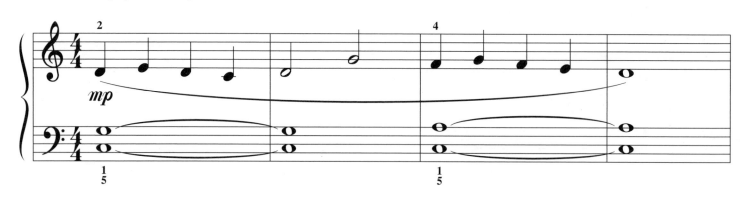

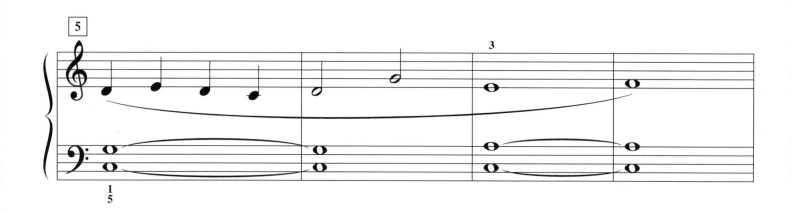

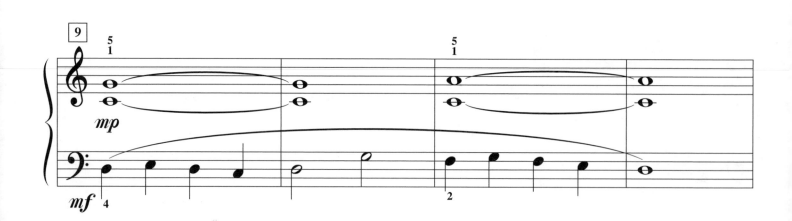

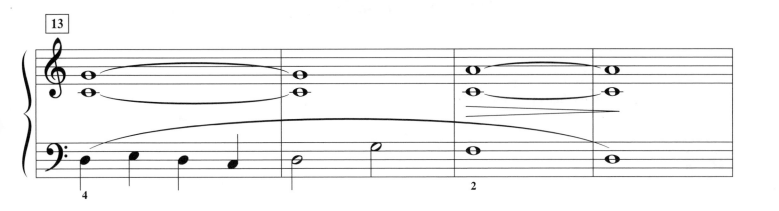

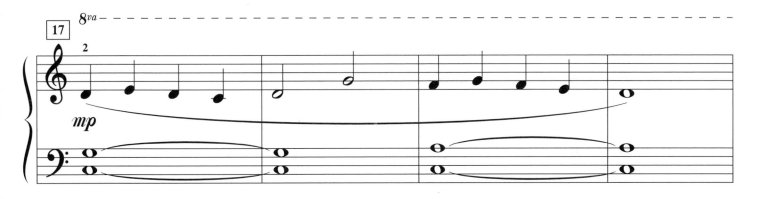

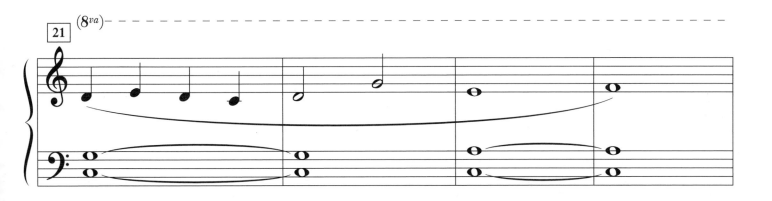

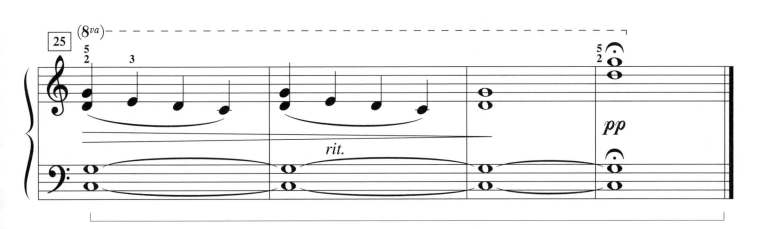

The Mad Scientist

With a very steady beat ($\quad$ = ca. 108)

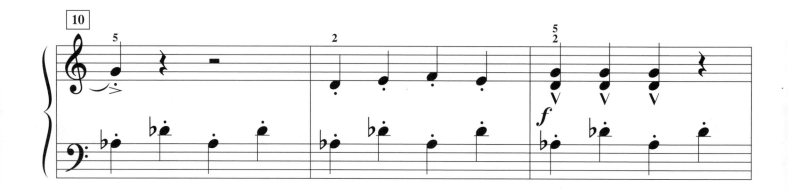

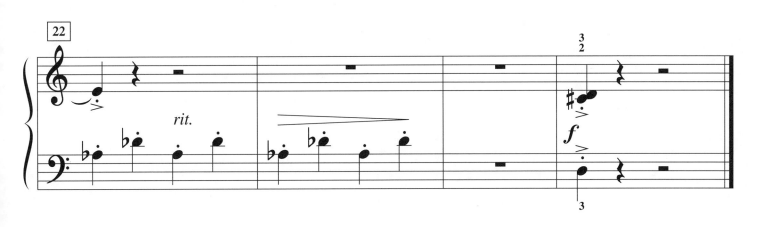

Waltz in Blue

Thoughtfully ($\dot{}$ = ca. 48)

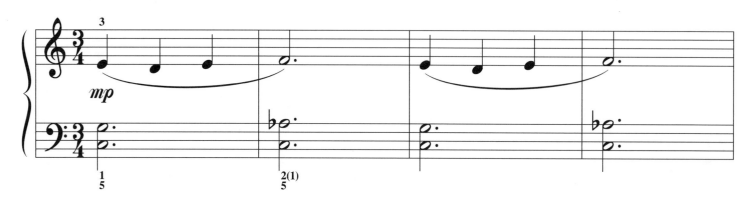

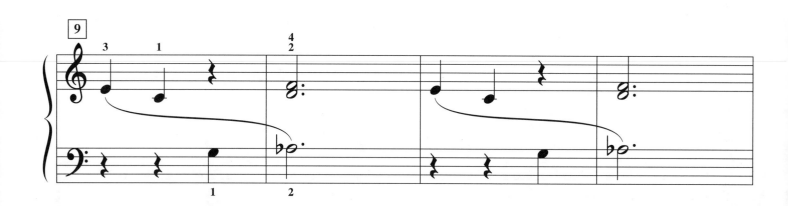

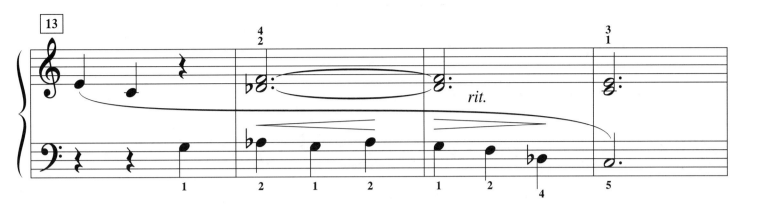

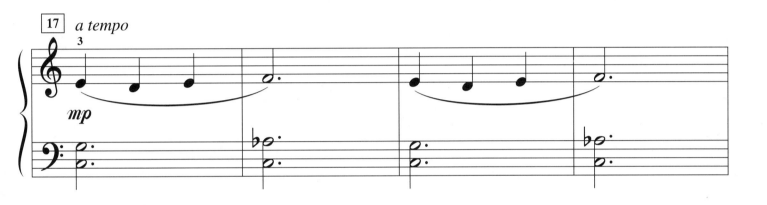

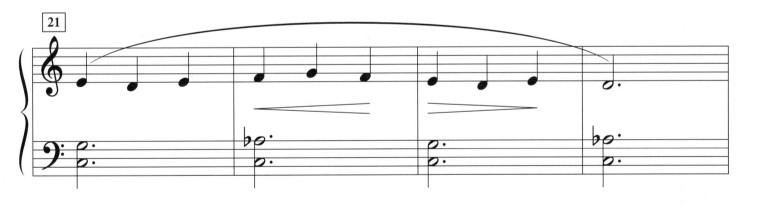

FF1318

The Barbarian

Heavy and rhythmic (♩ = 94 or faster)

Both hands 8ᵛᵃ lower throughout‐ ‐ ‐

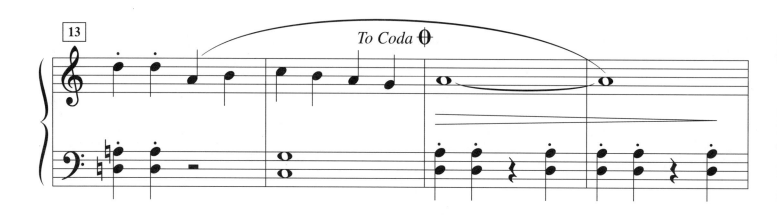

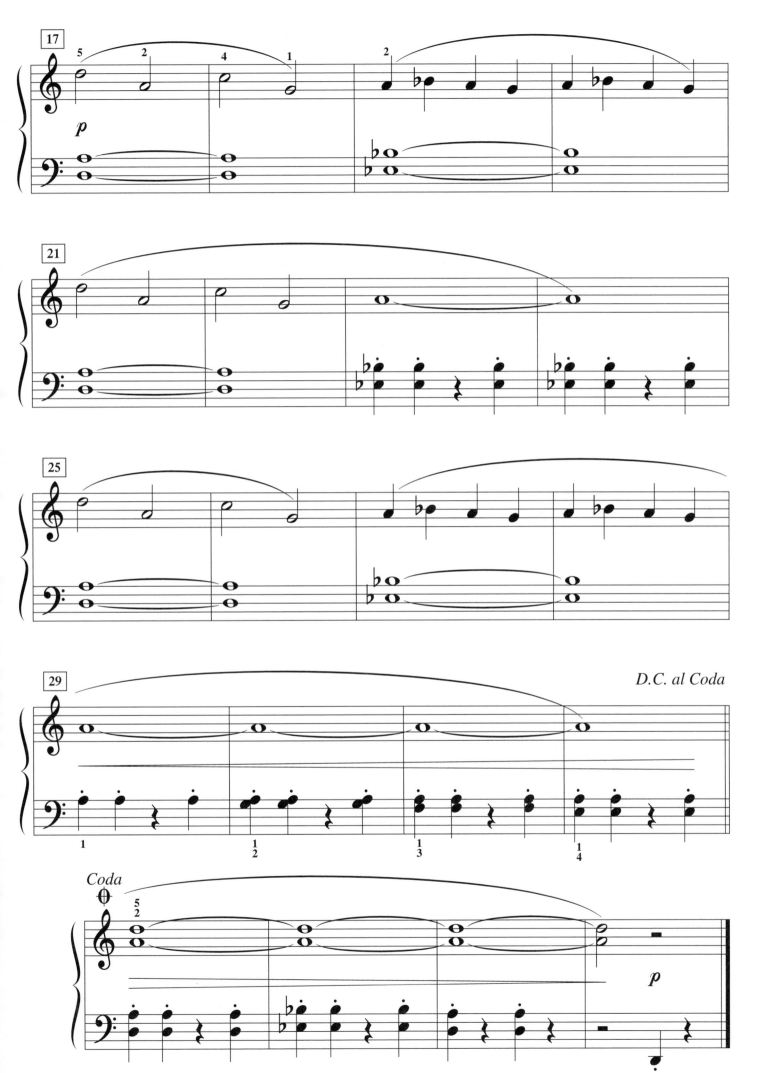

D.C. al Coda

Coda

Listening and Waiting

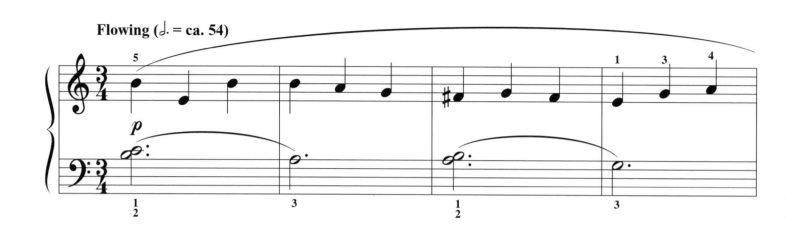

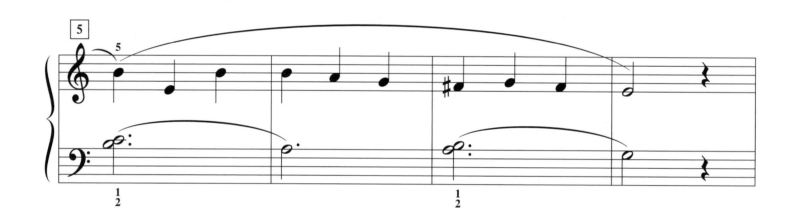

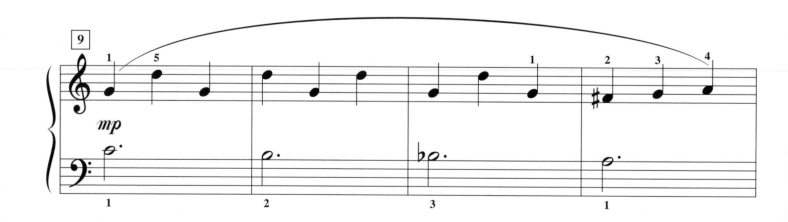

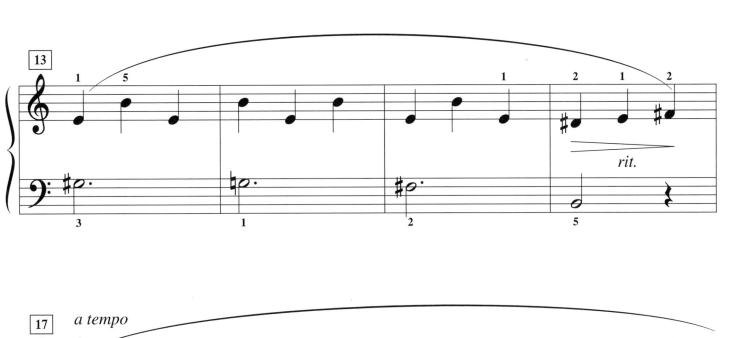

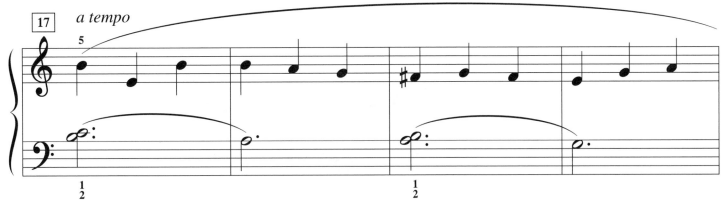

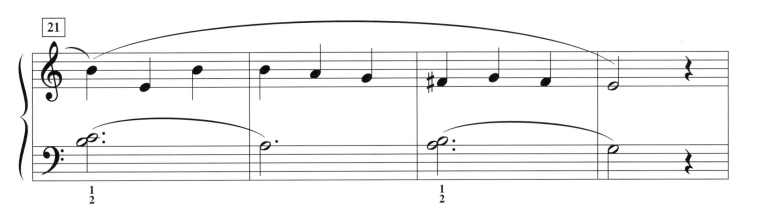

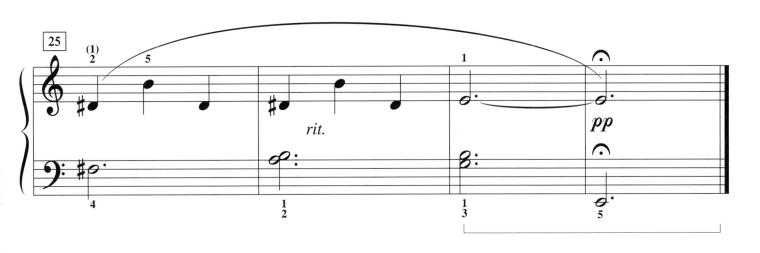